HIGHER EDUCATION GREEDY OVERRATED
AND OUTDATED
BY.
LEO HARDY

While every precaution has been taken in the preparation of this book, the publisher assumes no responsibility for errors or omissions, or for damages resulting from the use of the information contained herein.

HIGHER EDUCATION GREEDY OVERRATED AND OUTDATED

First edition. October 26, 2018.

Copyright © 2018 Leo Hardy.

Written by Leo Hardy.

CHAPTER ONE THE GREED OF MAJOR COLLEGES

It is greed to do all the talking but not to want to listen at all.- Democritus

Between 2005 and 2016, the cost of funding undergraduate education and boarding in America rose by 34 percent, indicated data from the U.S. Department of Education, National Center for Education Statistics. It is no wonder; therefore, that American students from wealthy families dominate the top universities! Research findings published in the Independent in 2014 show that teenagers from rich families have a 10 times better chance to enroll in top-notch colleges than the children from poor homes.

Even more worrying is the 2017 research finding that the most prestigious colleges in the United States have more learners from the 1 percent richest families than the bottom 60 percent, according to the New York Times. In 38 elite American colleges, including five Ivy League universities-Yale, Princeton, Dartmouth, Brown, and Penn, the majority of the students are from the top 1 percent income scale.

Statistics appearing in the New York Times depict a clear picture of how the super-rich dominate the population of 10 elite American colleges. In Washington University in St. Louis 21.7 of the undergraduates are from 6.1 the top percent families earning $630,000 dollars per year while only 6.1 percent come from the bottom 60% families earning less than $65,000 annually. At Colorado College, 24.2 percent from the richest homes, and only 10 percent from the low-income earners. At Colby College, it's 20.4 percent for the richest against 11.1 percent poor. The percentages of the 1 percent wealthy and 60 percent low-income groups at Trinity College (Conn.) are 26.2 vs 14.3, Bucknell University 20.4 vs 12.2, Colgate University 22.6 vs 13.6, Kenyon College 19.8 vs 12.2, and Middlebury College 22.8 vs 14.2.

In short, one of four students from rich families study in elite colleges. Approximately 40 percent of children from the top 0.1 percent income earners get their education in Ivy League Universities. However, only 0.5 percent of children from low income earners go to the top-ranked universities. Approximately 50 percent of the children whose homes have financial challenges do not attend college.

The outcome of this unfair arrangement is that most children who grow up poor become financially-deprived adults while most children from affluent families become wealthy adults!

Reason? The few poor students who receive education in elite colleges accumulate huge debts which they have to pay upon graduation.

Do these revelations shock you?

Yes, the statistics should disgust you because the cost of studies in top universities not only in America is beyond the reach of the youths from financially disadvantaged backgrounds. Consequently, there is a widening gap between the rich and the poor. The failure by teenagers whose parents are not financially endowed to join the best post-secondary school academic institutions means that the poor cannot easily achieve social mobility.

Why Poor Students Cannot Enroll in Top Universities

How come college education in the US exceptionally high yet some of the world's wealthiest universities are American? 94 American colleges have endowments over $1 billion. The Harvard University endowment fund is $36.4 billion, and in 2014 Harvard grew her fund by $565 million. As of 2015, the endowment funds in billion dollars at other major universities are as follows: Princeton University 22.72, Stanford University$22.22, Massachusetts Institute of Technology 13.47, The Texas A&M University 10.48, Northwestern University 10.19, University of Pennsylvania 10.13, and the University of Michigan 9.95.Corporate greed is the main reason higher education is unaffordable to the poor. Some top colleges have loads of money stashed in banks and prime property. There are universities that generate millions of dollars as untaxed income every year. For instance, from sports alone, Florida State University makes 123.3 million, University of South Carolina-$122.3 million, and Michigan State University — $100.9 million.

Ironically, the highly-ranked U.S. colleges increase tuition fees every year. In 2017, Penn University Board of Trustee hiked the fees from 68,000 to a confounding 71,200 covering the 2018-2019 academic year.

Still in 2017, Harvard announced a hike from $65,609 to $67,580. At Yale, the total cost of attendance is $66,900 from $69,430. Princeton's cost is $70,010, while at Cornell and Dartmouth, the increases are from $52,612 to $54,584 and $35,242 to $36,564 respectively for the undergraduates.

Nathan Lewis, who writes about tax and monetary policies for the Forbes Magazine, notes that fees in U.S. non-profit private colleges is about $50,000 a year. Lewis wonders where the money goes because an institution such as Colgate University has a $ 610 million endowment fund as well as donations and grants totaling $36 million annually. After analyzing the total costs of running the university, Lewis opines that Colgate only needs $62 million or 21,700 per student, which is only 44 percent of the fees Colgate University charges.

The Cost of Education in Major American Colleges

Ivy League institutions are the most preferred choice of post-high school education. Unfortunately, these elite higher learning campuses are among the most expensive. Often, the tuition charges in U.S. colleges involve five-digit numbers. A multinational banking and financial services firm, Hong Kong and Shanghai Banking Corporation (HSBC), in its 2017 report shows that parents typically contribute a whopping US$58,464 per year to fund a child's university education in the United States. The US$58,464 includes the tuition fees, books, transport, and accommodation. Quite a daunting task, isn't it?

As HSBC reveals, the amounts of money parents spend on their children's college education are too high and unaffordable to poor families.

HSBC has tabulated the average finances parents in selected countries spend on their child's education in U.S. dollars. Globally, parents pay an average of $44,221 to educate a child in university at undergraduate level. In the US, it is $58,464, China $42,892, Australia $36,402, Malaysia $25,479, UK $24,862, Canada $22,602, India $18,909, and France $16,708.

The Unfulfilled Career Dreams of Teenagers from Poor Families

Commenting on the HSBC survey, a University of Southampton scholar, Prof. Colin B. Grant, decries the fact that the huge finances required for college education deny the poor the opportunity to pursue high-flying careers, such as, medicine, engineering, technology, and accounting.

In the job market, because the children of the rich enroll in major colleges, the well-heeled students have a competitive advantage and can become highly-employable graduates. Most employers recognize the value of the graduates from the highly-ranked colleges. Thus, finances have a significant role in developing career skills. The rich homes can make the dreams of their children possible by financially supporting the children's education at the graduate and postgraduate levels. Contrariwise, disadvantaged financial statuses can frustrate the children of the poor aspiring to become highly-skilled and marketable professionals.

Tuition Fees at US Colleges-US $60,000 per Year!

The College Affordability and Transparency Center, a government department whose role is to provide the information about the U.S. universities charging the lowest and highest tuition fees estimates that educating a child in top-tier U.S. universities costs US $60,000 annually. After including the transport and living expenses, the College Board estimates that U.S. undergraduate colleges ask for the following finances in 2017/18:

- $17,580 at community colleges
- $25,290 at in-state four-year public colleges
- $40,940 at out-of-state four-year public colleges
- $50,900 at private, non-profit four-year colleges

The financially-disadvantaged cannot afford the education in the highly-ranked public colleges. At many prestigious U.S. public universities, the fees are equivalent to the amounts of money charged in private sector colleges. For instance, to study at the esteemed University of Michigan requires $47,476 for tuition alone. In addition to the tuition fees, students at the University of Michigan incur $11,198 for boarding, $2,454 for personal items, and $1,048 for educational supplies. This adds up to a total annual cost of $62,176 or $68,144 for graduate students.

The Astronomical $1.5 trillion Education Loan Burden

HIGHER EDUCATION GREEDY OVERRATED AND OUTDATED

Since college education in America is too expensive, millions of students from the working class have no choice but to borrow money so as to complete bachelor's degrees. The Department of Education reports that the indebted children come from the working as well as middle-class families. As of 2016, to complete a bachelor's degree required an average debt of $ $37,000, says the College Board. Nationwide, 44 million graduates jointly owe a monstrous $1.5 trillion as student-loan debt. In 2013, the debts amounted to $508.7 billion.

The student loan debts cannot be waived. The 2005 Bankruptcy Abuse Prevention and Consumer Protection Act classifies the education loan debts as the single non-dischargeable consumer debt in case of bankruptcy.

The indebted U.S. graduates and their families experience financial desperation: A whole generation is forced to deal with a lifetime debt and poverty, reveals the World Socialist Web. As a result of the average loan payments of about $393/month, the lives of the indebted graduates amount to misery in several ways:

• 14.4 percent of the loan holders are delinquents.• 39 percent of the 18-29-year-olds lack health insurance.• 24 percent move back home to stay with parents as the means to save money.• 22 percent of 18-34-year olds postpone having children.• 20 percent postpone their marriages.• 23 percent of the indebted graduates cannot afford basic necessities.• 49 percent take up jobs that they did not want so as to pay education loans.• 20 percent get into over $10,000 credit card debt traps.• The 22 percent of 18-34-year-olds push forward the dates to have children.

The College Education Loan Crisis in the United States

Most graduates borrow in order to complete Law, medicine, Master of Arts, Master of Business Administration, Master of Education, and Master of Science degrees. On average, graduate students borrow the finances listed below to complete college education.

- Law- $140,616
- Medicine and Health Science- $161,772
- Master of Arts- $58,539
- Master of Business Administration- $42,000
- Master of Education- $50,879,
- Master of Science- $50,400

The Student Education Loan Debt Collection Industry-Profitable and Parasitic Tendencies

Who benefits from the student loan debt? The massive finances involved in American education loans have turned debt collection into a lucrative business, argues MyDebt.com. Student loan servicers and debt collection agencies are big investments.

Borrowers do not get education loans directly from the Federal Government. Neither do the graduates send their loans payments to the U.S. Department of Education. There are loan servicers who act on behalf of the government by undertaking the following tasks:

- Processing and recording the payments.
- Certifying the borrowers' credentials.
- Loan collection.
- Assisting the borrowers to adjust loan payment plans.
- Billing.
- Approving the loan forbearance or deferment.

Approximately 45 percent of the American college students, or the current 44 million learners, take out loans. This is a huge financial consumer base, isn't it?

For every dollar that the 44 million students borrowed, the servicers will earn a slice from the interests and collection services. Currently, four servicers are in charge of the Federal Family Education Loans and federal direct loans. The main servicers are FedLoan Servicing (AES-PHEAA), Great Lakes Higher Education Corporation, Navient, and Nelnet.

Corporate Greed: Commission for the Servicers of College Education Debt

Whenever a student pays college education loan, the companies contracted to act for the U.S. Department of Education earn commissions, also known as contingent fee. The contractors' commission is usually 25 percent of the principal loan and interest paid by the borrower.

The Wall Street Profiteers

While explaining how Wall Street greed makes profits from student debt, reporter Raúl Carrillo says that "one person's debt is another person's asset." To Carrillo, profits from the education debts flow to third party investors. There is a circular money-making "student loan business complex" worth $200 billion. Lenders of college loans, such as Bank of America, Wells Fargo, and Sallie Mae are some of the big players in student loan asset-backed securities (SLABS).

Education debts are like home mortgages, stock exchange securities, and auto loans, reveals Carrillo. Big banks usually pool billions of dollars which they package as securities or innovative financial products. The banks then advertise the securities to investors. The investors who buy the securities receive interest from the monthly repayments. Investors can trade or even bet on the college loan securities.

Why Investors Love SLAB Investments

Student loan asset-backed securities attract investors because they are indestructible assets. With the government guaranteeing the loans and bankruptcy forbidden, Wall Street find the bets on college finances loss-proof. It's a guaranteed $1.5 trillion opportunity! Consider the massive interest rates charged on the student loans and you'll realize why the U.S. major colleges are for the real rich presently and in the future.

The Rich keep Getting Richer

Quite often, the wealthy lenders package state that the loans are for advancing the public good. However, the debts can further impoverish the low-income families, pupils of color, and, first-generation immigrants. Lenders, for example, CommonBond and SoFi, are competing to offer loans at 3.625% to 5.99% interest rates for five-year periods or 4.74% to 6.625% for ten-year durations. In all this corporate money-minting game, it is only the financiers who laugh all the way to the banks for raking in outrageous interests from college education debts. It's no brainer that only the real rich can afford the cost of getting an education from major colleges.

CHAPTER TWO HIGHER ACADEMIA IS NO HERO

HIGHER EDUCATION GREEDY OVERRATED AND OUTDATED

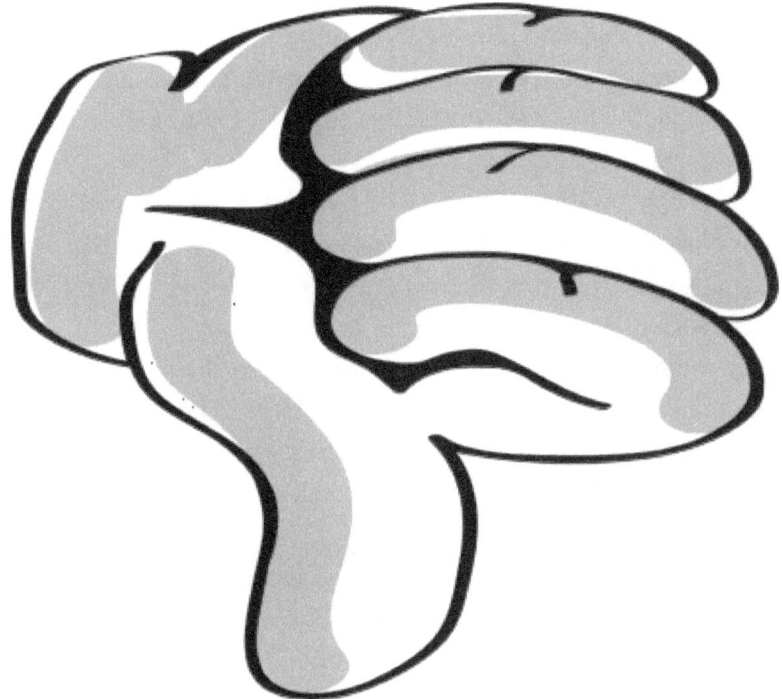

There was a theory years ago that when the United States ended its mandatory draft, the power shift would trade from the military and skills acquired there to getting a college degree. With a large influx of high school students about to enter the workforce something had to be done to delay that group from reaching the work sector for 4 years. If that theory is correct, then attendance at a four-year college was the answer to maintain the status quo. This solved a problem and created another. The students were delayed but the colleges across the country were given a lot of leeway on how they would conduct educating those students. With no real competition for students except between each other, colleges found ways to underperform and rise the price of tuition.

The large pool of students prior to the ending of the mandatory draft, colleges had to be good and they had to keep their costs low. Afterall, there were fewer students to choose between. With the ending of the draft, colleges were able to write their own tickets and design their degree programs anyway they wanted. Because of the large pool of students, they could also raise their tuition up to make sure they made money. They had an endless supply of students and few regulations governing their behavior.

Degree programs did not have to be relevant or educational, they just needed to recruit or admit enough students to cover their costs and make a profit. Educating the students and preparing them for life was not a priority.

If they are not educating them for this reason then why do colleges cost so much? That is a good question. Here are several reasons why the tuition rates are so high:
- Aesthetics not education- many colleges have focused on providing the luxuries in life and have sacrificed education to do so.

Modern dorm rooms, top rated dining facilities, and attractive commons areas are the focus now.
- Bloated faculty and staff- colleges invented new positions that needed to be filled. These positions have little to do with education and simply follow popular cultural features.

The need to score high- when a college moves up in the college rankings, they get more students. They are not focusing on education because they want to look good to those who compose those rankings.

Prestige means money- The status of a college means more than the actual students who attend. The better the prestige the more money they can charge tuition. It is not the education that counts but the prestige that follows the student when they hunt for jobs.

Faculty research programs- someone has to fund the professors' academic interests and equipment. States aren't doing it as they have cut back on their support to colleges. Also, if a faculty member makes that one big discovery, the college gets more press, more prestige and more students.

HIGHER EDUCATION GREEDY OVERRATED AND OUTDATED

Cutting edge technology- colleges need to keep current with the latest technological advances. If they don't then they could possibly lose a lot of students. If the college loses students, they go down in the rankings and lose prestige. They may not be able to attract top faculty researchers to get that status back.

Athletics- coaches do not come cheap anymore. At least for the men's basketball and football teams. You cannot expect the college to pay those salaries out of their own pockets now. These two teams generate a lot of revenue, but heaven forbid if that money is shared with other student groups or academics.

Do colleges prepare their students

We would not be so arrogant and say that all colleges underperform and fail to prepare their students for the real world. But we would also not be so naïve to think that there are many who do. Times have changed, and the focus of colleges have changed as well. There used to be a time when colleges actually did prepare their students and educated them properly. But with the changing attitudes of today and the past few decades, making students feel good, feel normal, and other priorities education seems to have been put on the back burner.

Some students complain that they are being trained to meet the standards of the 20th century and not the 21st. They are being taught to dress correctly, shake hands properly and make standard resumes.

What the students are looking for is to be trained in how to network right, how to obtain strategic internship appointments, and other 21st century skills. They do not like the fact that they have to hire other professionals once they graduate to get the skills they should have gotten in college

One-way colleges are failing their students

It seems that some colleges have engaged in a war on teaching and teachers for some time now. For some reason, the popular and good teachers who have not reached their tenure promotion have been fired. With this threat hanging over their heads, many college professors go on the offensive. They attack the public school system, saying that they are not preparing their students for college life. But this strategy fails to address the issue of teacher firings. That could be because these same complaining professors are the ones educating the public school teachers. They are merely seeing the results of their handiwork.

The core issue

As we have seen there are numerous reasons why colleges are underperforming and seek to get high pay for inferior quality work. The real reason for all of this boils down to one important fact. Even though these colleges exist to teach students, they have a bad attitude towards teaching. This charge is long, loud and comes from many places. Change the attitude and you may see a difference in how colleges perform. If we are lucky, then we may see a return to the original roots for the existence of colleges. We may see them return to educating their students and making education the priority it should be. The right teaching will improve any school.

CHAPTER THREE COLLEGE DROPOUT

College Dropout Rate

The word dropout rate means, the number of students not completing a particular college or school course. The current rate of dropout is one per three students. Every year 1.2 million students drop out of the college, in the United States of America alone.

Reasons for dropping out of college

Many Americans attend their college studies with the determination of achieving their planned goals. However, many students are prone to unprecedented challenges while in college. The research has proved that 44 million Americans hold more than 1.4 trillion as student loan debt.

Only 54.8 million students eventually graduate in six years. Therefore, this shows that many American students are having huge education loan debt, without any degree or diploma to show. Typically, the dropout rate is nothing short of tragic. Therefore, it important to address it since many students are not graduating as expected. On the other hand, many parents have raised concerns, saying the system is too expensive and takes long before graduating a few students.

College Dropout Statistics

It has been proven that one-third of the entire students joining a college, normally drop out. During the six years course, statistics have proved that only half of the students complete and graduate. Although money is considered as the backbone of the college dropout problem, other factors also contribute. Below are some of these factors:

1.) Social life:

Generally, overdoing it at the college comes with some consequences. Excessive late night parties and drinking too much alcohol, make it difficult to continue with the college. Typically, these affect the dropout in three major different ways:

• Most parents become discouraged and stop paying school fees for their children. Actually, they consider it as the waste of money or resources.

HIGHER EDUCATION GREEDY OVERRATED AND OUTDATED

- The common type of punishment that many colleges have adopted is expelling students from the college due to academic failure.
- Some students choose to drop out of college, after failing several classes.

2.) Remedial college courses

When a student takes a remedial course in college, affects the graduation. Actually, it increases the bills for tuition. Generally, less than one-fourth of the entire students, required to have remedial courses complete the program and graduate.

3.) Failing to balance

It is a challenge for many students that work while attending their classes. They find it difficult to balance responsibility and college. Additionally, they also consider it as being costly and takes longer to graduate.

Consequences of dropping out

Typically, when a student drops out of college, then he is likely to be unemployed. Many graduates do not have a hard time looking for a job. This is because all employers are looking for people with a higher diploma than that of high school. If a drop out had student loans or grants, these might result in more debt within a short time.

The drop out might also lose the grace period given to repay the education loan. Some of the colleges will require you to repay them directly, for the tuition while you attended. If the only option left is to drop out, it is important to consider the college dropout policy. The student can as well consult the school management before leaving.

Despite the financial consequences, personal or family problems affect the students. A family that has many conflicts can affect the student mentally. They result in low self-esteem, which affects their studies.

Bottom line

It is very important for a student to be careful, before accepting any college invitation. Find out about their graduation rates. Consider a college that you can afford college fees, in order to avoid the added pressure that may make you to consider dropping out of college.

It is very important to offer mental and physical assistance to the student unfortunately most colleges do not do this. They should be guided and informed about the journey of college life accordingly.

CHAPTER FOUR COLLEGE VS. TRADE SCHOOL

Education is important

That is one of the important messages you have been told by your parents and your high school teachers. You need a good education to get ahead and be successful. It seems that the adults of this world have all gotten together and deemed a one size fits all education is best for

HIGHER EDUCATION GREEDY OVERRATED AND OUTDATED

everyone. Unfortunately, a one size fits all education plan is not the best strategy. There are alternatives which may fit more people better and still help them be successful. Trade schools provide a good education as well as training their students in specific industries. Students that go to good trades schools can be just as successful and just as happy with their lives as their college bound counterparts.

The drawbacks of attending college

Everyone likes to focus on the good things a college degree provides.•

A college degree opens doors•

A college degree helps you earn more money•

A college degree educates you. But all is not perfect with a college education. Here are some of the drawbacks that come with attending college over a trade school:•

It takes at least 4 years- in order to get your degree, you need to stay in school an additional 4 years. Sometimes it can take 5• Tuition is not cheap- you are looking at over $100,000 on average to pay for your degree• Graduate in debt- Most college students have to take out student loans to pay for their education. These students are already behind the 8 ball when the graduate and have to work harder to become debt free.• Studying is hard work- if you thought you had it tough during high school, that was a walk in the park when it comes to college. Many students aren't ready for the hard work and drop out.• Employment placement- depending on your course of study and degree program you may not get that dream job and have to take lesser paying work to get by.

There are alternatives

Attending college and getting your degree is not all bad. There are a lot of good points that come with attending college. But a 4-year program may not be for you. Not everyone is cut out to be an academic. You may have other interests that the regular brick and mortar schools do not address effectively. One alternative to college is a good trade school. They know that not everyone can or wants to go to college. They design their curriculums to focus on educating their students where it is most important. The following lets you know what trade schools are about:• Teach skills for specific jobs•

Develop specific skill sets for those jobs•

Provided concentrated education on specific jobs•

Provide hands on opportunities to develop your confidence• Provide you with a variety of job opportunities•

Help you develop so you can advance and grow in your career.

The benefits of going to trade schools

While trades schools do not get the press that regular colleges get, there are some great benefits to attending a trade school for your education. You can get ahead of the game by choosing to attend a trade school over a traditional 4-year college:

1. You save time- your education is completed in two years instead of the usual four.

2. Great employment opportunities- skilled workers are in high demand. This means you may have better and more job openings to choose between.

3. You save money- The average tuition for a 4-year college runs around $125,000. The average tuition for a good trade school reaches about $30,000

4. Less debt-it is easier to become debt free and spend your money on the things you want to buy.

5. Smaller class size- you can get more attention from the instructor and ask your questions a lot easier. You also get to know your fellow students better making for better friendships.

6. Hands on training- in a trade school you get work experience, not just head knowledge. This helps put you ahead of the students in traditional colleges.

7. Multiple application deadlines- trade schools offer many different times where you can apply and start your education. You may only have

to wait a few weeks to start your education if you miss one application deadline.

8. Employment help- once enrolled you get help with your resume, communication skills, learn how to network and much more. You also get help in finding a job. You are not left to navigate the professional employment area alone

9. Job security- The training you receive is very difficult to send overseas for cheaper labor. As older workers retire, you will find more opportunities for work.

10. Good salary- on average a graduate of a trade school can expect, within reason and on average, to earn in the neighborhood of about $35,000 a year. It all depends on the skill of the worker and the employment market

Why should you consider a trade school?

There are a variety of reasons why you should consider attending a trade school over a traditional college. The benefits listed above are just part of the reasons why you should consider your educational alternatives. There is one more benefit that may finally convince you. The general education you receive at a traditional college isn't limited to those institutions. When you complete your trade school training, you can always buy books, read magazines, attend different lectures and seminars to upgrade your education.

A good student is always learning, and you can learn as much as a student of a regular college. The difference is you can pay for that education from the salary you are already earning from your trade school education. You do not have to go into debt to be educated. The only thing that stops you from being educated is you. Trade schools only make it easier for you to reach your educational and career goals.

Some final thoughts.

Attending a traditional 4-year college is not wrong. These academic institutions do a fine job in educating their students. Unfortunately, they just are not the right fit for everyone. Going to a trade school can give you an edge in employment, debt reduction ad a lot more. It also helps you become better educated in the career you want to pursue. A good trade school is a great alternative when you want more out of life than just a 4-year diploma.

CHAPTER FIVE DEBT AND MORE DEBT

Many people complete high school with prospects of joining college. However, not everyone has wealthy parents who have the college costs covered or great scholarships that allow them to study debt free. That means that several people are forced to consider getting their college education on debt. These debts seem like an obvious way to achieve your goal and you're going to be earning enough to pay it anyway right? The sad news is that in truth it is not always that easy. There are one too many horror stories of people up to their neck in debt. These are huge debts that go up to hundreds of thousands of dollars. Getting student loans is easy and it feels great to get that money and see yourself progressing with peers.

For many people, reality strikes the moment the first deduction has to be made. You realize that first, you make much less than you anticipated, your debt is possibly gaining interest and your monthly contribution is but a drop in the bucket. So the main question you should ponder is, are student loans really worth it? You will find a lot of advice online on ways to manage student loans and ways to make the load lighter. However, few of these mostly unqualified "financial advisers" will tell you the truth behind these loans. Spending money you don't have yet is never a good idea. Regardless of what you might think is a very legitimate way.

So what are some of the biggest drawbacks to getting student loans?

They are very expensive

To study in a top college in the US, most of which are nonprofit private institutions, can cost up to 60,000 dollars for one year. A public college will cost an average of about 25,000 dollars for an undergraduate degree per year. This amount of debt for someone who is yet to begin their career is insane and will be inadvisable in any other platform. It is equally insane that this type of debt for someone starting out on life is normalized and even advised.

Getting the money and paying your student fees can fill you with hope of a bright future. It is not often that people will consider that each passing year is more money out of your pocket in your already uncertain future.

Student loans gain interest. So now that you already have a huge loan to pay off, how about paying some extra cash while at it? Some people are so deep in student loan debt all the money they have been paying off is the debt their loans have acquired over the years and the principal (actual money you spent) stays untouched. Talk about a vicious cycle.

Before running out to get your first student loan check and remember you might just have to pay a lot more extra in future in money you have not even earned just yet. The reason many people are suffering bad credit scores is because they barely realized that the interest kept going up and they now have to pay more than the amount they thought they would initially.

If you really have to take the student loan, ensure you are aware of the rates and do some basic calculation on how much you will be expected to pay. You must repay even if you don't complete studies.

Have you considered yet that you might change your mind before you finish your studies? If you don't, there is a possibility you might fail your classes. These are two reasons among hundreds that cause people to drop out or get kicked out of college. The risks incurred in getting a student loan is immeasurable. There is no special consideration for people who are unable to achieve their initial goal when they first started out in college.

Before getting that loan just yet, keep in mind that if things went wrong, you will still be expected to pay off your debt. This might be a huge cost to pay for failure and uncertainty. Unfortunately, credit is credit and you owe someone for your incomplete degree and you deserve to know the reality before jumping head first into debt.

You might have to forfeit interests. So what happens to people who have loans to pay off? Great question because the answer is they have to pay it off. As a young person starting out in life, a student loan will be a dark cloud looming over your head. This means that to afford paying back this debt and afford a decent lifestyle, you might just have to cut out many costs.

Paying off a student loan in many cases can take twenty five years and even more. That is a long time to be in debt. That is without considering credit card debts that many people have and mortgages that many people also have to pay. Getting extra money for hobbies and other interests might become downright impractical.

Let's mention bad credit scores? If you are a living breathing human being, you must know by now that life is very unpredictable. In fact nothing ever happens exactly how you see it in your head. That is reason enough to make you think twice about any kind of credit. You may have expectations of completing college and getting a great job that pays you well and paying off you student loans becomes a breeze and you live large and travel the world.

Sounds great, only problem is that you might get pregnant immediately after college and have to provide for someone else, or break your arms in a freak accident and be unable to work for a while. This might cause people to be unable to keep up with their monthly payment. This causes your credit scores to go down and it affects how much lenders can give you in future when you need to borrow again.

This kind of doom may not befall you. However, you can tell that student loans can be a huge burden and it's likely you will be in debt for many years. A college education can definitely not be understated in this cut throat society. It is advisable to weigh your options and try to find the solution that makes you have the least debt possible.

CHAPTER SIX WHY THE COLLEGE EDUCATION SYSTEM ISN'T WORKING

HIGHER EDUCATION GREEDY OVERRATED AND OUTDATED

In the past century going to college was a great step and it acted as stepping stone towards a successful life. However, the idea of having a degree resulted to automatic success in life is now a scam and many who follow it to end up in catastrophic failure.

In the past decade, the cost for an annual tuition was 17000 dollars. At the moment it is 44750 dollars per year without forgetting the one thousand million dollars (one billion)that the government has invested in students loan who will inevitably be underemployed, unemployed and will likely never be in a position to pay the loan. Instead of the cost of education reducing due to the advancement of technology, research has shown that student loan is now greater than credit and mortgage debts combined!

What aggravates the situation even further is that, current employers are evaluating candidates less on what they scored and more on experience or portfolio. Many have been disappointed walking in a well-established company, wide-eyed and green with a bachelors degree at the age of 22 only to be turned down. The current world need someone smart who have walked the walk, knows what life is and is capable of coming up with something out nothing. The bubble caused by the student loan will result in a considerable drop in school tuition and finally the collapse of higher education system down the line. The bitter truth is that parents want that "degree" for their kids to be successful. Statistics show that nearly 85% of students will go home jobless and start hustling for money to pay for the loan the government granted them. That's hard to believe, right? Ultimately one is left indebted and is forced to live in the mom's basement for a majority of their hustling life.

What does all this translates into?

Young people need to start reasoning of opportunities instead of putting all their hopes in academic success.It hurts to see fresh an unprepared graduates dive in denial as they are faced with the bitter truth. The next thing they think is "I am going to get a masters to better my opportunities" only for them to waste three years and extra money.

THE COLLEGE WON'T TEACH YOU HOW TO BE SUCCESSFUL, TRUE?

The biggest illusion that the colleges and universities have managed to sell to the public is self application. The song is the same, go to college and you'll have a good life." They never tell you there is need for freedom, need for maturity, need for leadership and society skills, need for honoring passion and personal drive, need to learn negotiation skills and need to flow with the current situation. For them the die is cast, just follow the yellow brick road and you will be there. A great deception.

In the current world success is all about integrity, self-control, self development, passion and most importantly successful people who can be your mentor and show you the right path. Remember, at any point passion always beats talent.

THE PRESSING LOAN ISSUE.

The main problem does not lay with the 4 years graduates but with the school dropout who are left with no knowledge and are expected to pay back the loan. Those who are considered lucky and get themselves some sort of job cannot save even ten percent of their earnings. This prepares a platform for a miserable old age. With nothing to show for the years and money spent, the youth may quickly fall into criminal activities due to rage and desperation. Just as the proverb says the rich rule the poor, so does the borrower is a servant to the lender. The period of young adulthood was meant for building and not digging oneself out of a hole. The heavy debt burden has also pushed children and marriages away as one fill he or she is not ready to be committed to both. Studies show people start living a meaningful portion of life at the early 40s as at this period the debt to income ratio is considerable, and they can buy a house and maybe start a family.

SLOW ADAPTING COLLEGE INSTITUTIONS.

HIGHER EDUCATION GREEDY OVERRATED AND OUTDATED

It is pure logic that a firm will employ a person with 4 years of experience rather than a lad with a resume of 4 years of college. The rigid education system makes it almost impossible for the colleges to switch the curriculum before it changes all over again due to the varying trends. Managers have learnt this, and they normally look for three things to employ.

Experience. Who does the employee know, who have they worked for, how long have they been in the industry and the ultimate question is how much have you achieved.

Portfolio. The new employer will want tangible evidence of what you claim to have achieved.

Personality

If you do not rhyme perfectly with the culture of the company and the potential customers, life is going to get even harder. Another pressing issue is that many students are forced to take courses which they do not love, the main excuse being that they are prestigious. One end up developing chronic depression as one is forced to do what he or doesn't like. It is better to work for 60 hours a day doing what you love rather 40 doing what you hate. It is also fair to make less and have no loan debts rather than make a considerable amount which is then swept away by creditors. The truth is that colleges and higher learning institution will not teach you how to be successful and how to start and learn a business. Their main mentality is for you to graduate and go work for somebody else.

BOTTOM LINE.

The issues affecting the education system are not going to be solved overnight using a magic bullet. It is important for parent and students to look for other alternatives because at the moment, considering the level of technology advancement, the time spent should be approximately half of the four years. The society should also stop judging the success of their kids based on their grades but rather on knowledge, skills gained and experience.

Did you love *Higher Education greedy Overrated and Outdated*? Then you should read *Evil Games That Should Not Be Played* by Leo Hardy!

Charlie Charlie, The Hosting Game, Ouija boards, The Midnight Game and a few more are covered in this book.There are games that have proven to be too dangerous to play and we are not talking about games that involve fast cars, driving, bullets or wild animals, but games that involve the supernatural. Games like Tarot, Ouija, The Hosting Game and countless others were contacting spirits have been around for centuries. These games have been causing supernatural infestations for years as well. Despite warnings from those who have played them and members of the clergy people continue to play these games.In my book Evil Games That Should not be Played, you will learn the rules and hazards of some of the most dangerous occult games on earth. The game Charlie Charlie has caused mass hysteria in a group of girls that played it. One Man Hide and Seek may be the creepiest game that I have ever researched and countless haunting and satanic incidences can be traced back to the use of spirit and or Ouija boards. Also, you will read about herbs, charms, and talismans used to defend against evil spirits and the cleansing ceremonies that can get rid of them. I hope that you will read about the games in this book, but I strongly suggest that you play none of them. More than your life may be at risk if you do. You have been warned.

Also by Leo Hardy

evil book trilogy
Evil Book Trilogy Complete Three Book Set

higher education
Higher Education greedy Overrated and Outdated

mental illness
Depression Dealing With Depression

PARANORMAL INVESTIGATORS
Paranormal Investigators 5 Gaurav Tiwari Death of a Ghost Hunter
Paranormal Investigators 8, Harry Houdini and Sir Arthur Conan Doyle
Paranormal Investigators 10 Paranormal Pioneers and The Modern Investigator
Paranormal Investigators The Collection Books 6 - 10

www.ingramcontent.com/pod-product-compliance
Lightning Source LLC
Chambersburg PA
CBHW031556210526
45464CB00003B/1311